SEADOGS, CLOWNS, and GYPSIES

The Best-- And the Worst!-- of Cap'n Fatty

**Twenty Sea Stories about
Colorful Caribbean Characters,
Wonderful Waterfront Wackos,
and Lush Tropical Vegetables!**

by

Gary "Cap'n Fatty" Goodlander

Dedication:

To Jim Long of CARIBBEAN BOATING for being the first person crazy enough to pay for my writing.

To Marty Luray of SAIL for buying my first 'real' manuscript.

To my wife Carolyn for putting up with such a massive amount of personal, financial, and sea-going abuse.

And to David Lovik for making it all possible.

Thanks!

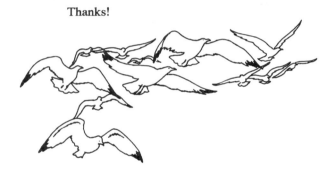

(ISBN 0-9631060-2-3)

Cover Design: Keryn Bryan of KATYDIDS

Fourth printing September 1993

Editor's Note: The stories "The Last Cruise" and "Sailing to Nowhere" previously appeared in SAIL magazine. "The Fox of Jost Van Dyke" was originally published in CHARTERING. Both "How to Spot a Maxi Racer" and "Chartering Pioneers" first appeared in the MARINE SCENE. In a shorter form, "Baby Aboard" appeared in SAILING. Most of the other stories (or portions thereof) originally were published in CARIBBEAN BOATING.

Table of Contents

PREFACE

These stories-- culled from hundreds of manuscripts I've written in the last few years-- were never intended to be compiled into a book. They were dashed off solely to make money. I prefer writing to honest labor.

But looking back, I realize they collectively tell a unique story. The Seadogs, Clowns, and Gypsies who inhabit these pages are among the freest, most creative, and most entertaining people on our watery plant.

I am honored to sing their praises.

One other thing-- I have resisted the temptation to rewrite these stories for a number of reasons. Many of them have a late-night-this-must-be-at-the-printer-in-the-morning tone which I find refreshing. I do not take myself or my work too seriously. I send these stories out into the world like flawed children-- knowing they are not perfect, praying they will succeed despite my influence, and loving each wholeheartedly.

Mind the Rudder
Or Meet the Rock,

Cap'n Fatty Goodlander

THE LAST CRUISE

"Carlotta" ghosted along at dusk in the Gulfstream. The wind had gone down with the sun, and it was that quiet time between the death of the day and the rebirth of night. Carolyn, my wife and fellow sailor for the past 14 years, puttered at the galley sink. Roma Orion, our three year old daughter (who had twenty stamps in her passport on her first birthday), sat beside me in the cockpit. She waited expectantly for her nightly bedtime story.

I took a deep breath and began. "When I was a child, I lived on 'Elizabeth' with my mommy and my daddy and my two sisters. And if I was good, my daddy would let me sit in the cockpit at night, and he would tell me stories about fishing and sailing and swimming. And about how the stars tell you where you are and how each ocean wave contains answers to many questions..."

"Your dad..." she said.

"Yes. My dad, your grandpa Jim. Remember? In the hospital?"

She said nothing, but I could tell that she remembered. She had been afraid of the thin palsied hand that had reached out between the white sheets to embrace her.

Carolyn stood framed in the companionway, backlit by the

3

soft glow of the kerosene cabin lamps. "Give your dad a hug-kiss, Roma," Carolyn said. "I'll tell you a story below. Your dad's... tired."

I steered all night, not bothering with the electric autopilot or the windvane. Sleep never entered my mind. Carolyn came up a few times and offered to take a watch, but I turned her down. I wanted to be alone with only my boat and my thoughts. I wanted to talk to my father one last time.

"Listen to the boat, son," he had told me long ago. "Ask the boat what she wants. Fools command ships, sailors guide them. A good boat is smarter than you'll ever be. The Art of Sailing is one of listening, asking, understanding. Never fight the boat; never attempt to 'beat' the sea. Accommodate them. Cooperate. Learn from them..."

His nickname was "The Guru." I remember when he earned it. During one of our annual haul-outs, "Elizabeth", a 52-foot schooner, was next to an old yawl that had just been purchased by some college kids. A whole gang of them were working on her furiously. They were bringing her down to bare wood. It wasn't until they had her all primed and ready for the finish coats that they realized that they had ground off the boot top stripe and had no idea where the waterline went.

They came to my father for advice. "No problem," he said. "Give me the paint..."

He started at the bow on the starboard side, working his way aft. By amidships, they were concerned. "It has to be level from side to side," said one.

"And straight as an arrow, or it will look awful," said another.

"And, of course, it has to join up at the bow..." said a third.

My father said nothing. A commercial artist and sign painter by profession, his very eye was a straight edge. Around the other side of the boat he went, and when he reached the bow, the lines joined perfectly.

"The Guru," one of them said and jokingly fell to his knees. The name stuck. And the fact that I'd secretly helped him mark the waterline before they had ground it off didn't make him less of a "Guru" in my book, but more of one.

He loved to joke, carrying a mannequin's hand in the back pocket of his baggy shorts, tossing it to anyone working as we made our daily dock rounds, saying, "Here, let me give ya a hand..."

He wasn't famous. He never circumnavigated. He never wrote a best-selling cruising guide. But he was well liked and respected wherever cruising boats gathered in the Gulf and along the East Coast, the Mississippi River, or the Great Lakes.

"Elizabeth," designed by Alden and built by Morse in 1919, wasn't in yacht-perfect shape. He preferred sailing and playing with his kids to endless maintenance.

He bought his first boat at 16 years of age. It cost more to hire a team of horses to drag it to his backyard than to purchase it. His own father said, "It will never float."

It did. And I have faded pictures of them smiling together in the cockpit as she sailed along with a bone in her teeth. My father, looking at the camera from the tiller, looked as happy as any man can be.

A few years before his death, a wonderful thing happened to him. Walking down a dock, he spotted a boat that he had owned. He hadn't seen her in over forty years. She looked better than when he had sold her.

A young man was wiping down her varnish and noticed him staring at the boat. "Hello," my father said, "I used to own her."

"I don't think so," said the young man kindly. "She has been in my family for almost 50 years. The only man that ever owned her besides us was her builder, James E. Goodlander."

"You can call me Jim," said my father. "May I come aboard?"

When Carolyn and I built our 36-foot ketch, "Carlotta", over the course of five long, hard years, we often called him for advice. "Dad, how long should I make the chainplates?" I was 19 years old when I started.

"Have you ever sailed on a boat with chainplates that were too long or too strong..." he asked. He was like that, often answering a question with a question, allowing you to come up with your own answers. He forced you to think it through.

All of his life was spent upon the sea, learning from it, listening to it, seeking always to understand it better. When we cruised as a family in the 1950's, we were an oddity. Newspapers wrote stories about us, radio stations interviewed us, magazines sent reporters. The same question was repeated over and over. "Where are you headed next?"

And my father's answer was always the same. "See there," he'd say, pointing out to sea. "See the horizon? Well, just over the horizon, just a little further than we can see, is something so beautiful and pure, that I will spend my whole life traveling to see it..."

Once a reporter, missing the point entirely, asked, "And when do you expect to arrive?"

"Never," my father said. "I hope."

He never sailed his last boat. He was too ill to even consider it. But even so, she was his main interest in life after his family.

Near the end, he fell overboard and didn't have the strength to pull himself back aboard. For hours he hung on a dockline, yelling weakly until someone came to rescue him. Everyone thought it was terrible that his family didn't stop such a dangerous practice by such an obviously ill man. We didn't dare. And wouldn't have even if we could.

Finally, while attempting to nail some small item to a bulkhead, he realized that he didn't have the strength to lift the hammer. "Sell her," he told my mother that evening. And he never saw his beloved "Marie" again.

Growing up on the "Elizabeth" was like growing up in a fairy tale. The world was our oyster, the boat safe harbor, the family our universe. The world was a simple and just place. People were good and true and faithful. The laws of Mother Nature were fair, if unforgiving. There was a time to joke and a time to reef, a time to soak up the sun and a time to endure the frigid North wind at the helm. A very good time.

And now I am raising my own daughter aboard, attempting

6

to give her at least a taste of the wonderful childhood with which I was blessed.

I suddenly sat upright in "Carlotta's" cockpit. Off the port bow was a misshapen orange disk-- like a molten deformed dinner plate. It was dawn. Everything was perfectly still-- as if the sea was holding it's breath. Waiting.

I rushed below and grabbed the urn.

His ashes were surprisingly heavy. Multi-colored and textured. I said some words-- words too private to repeat in print. I poured him into the deep blue waters of the Gulf Stream to voyage endlessly and eternally. I set him free on his last cruise.

And as I poured his ashes into the sea, for an instant the world shifted and I saw the future. And it was not my hand pouring my father, but my child's hand pouring me into the ocean. I was over-come with a feeling of wholeness and goodness such as I had never experienced before.

As I watched the ashes disappear astern, a gentle wind heeled "Carlotta." She started chuckling along, heading for the Lesser Antilles a thousand miles away.

The world was still a true and just place. Mother Nature was still fair, if unforgiving. People were still good.

And I was blessed with a fine sailing breeze.

"Good-bye, Dad," I whispered into the wind.

Welcome to Paradise, Eliza!

White Bay, Jost Van Dyke, BVI-- A fine time was had by all at a recent christening party for young Eliza Marie Callwood. The party, held at White Bay on Jost Van Dyke, was widely attended by both Josters and their many St. Johnian sailing friends. The proud parents-- Godwin Callwood and Maria Cimonetti-- welcomed arriving guests on the beach as each arrived by dinghy. There was a mountain of West Indian food, plenty of Reggae music loud enough to awake Brother Bob from the dead, and an endless river of rum...

Maria's parents-- revelling in their newly discovered role as international grandparents-- flew into St. Thomas from Vermont and chartered a bareboat to attend the party. Afterwards, the entire family-- including Eliza Marie-- sailed off to Virgin Gorda, where Godwin taught Grandfather Bill Cimonetti some of the finer points of "liming 'round de Islands, Mon," and the women made goo-goo eyes at the new baby.

The Christening Party itself was enlivened further by the antics of a large power yacht chartered by a crew of wild and crazy folks from New Orleans who just happened to be cruising by.

The boat turned out to be both Louisiana crewed and Louisiana crude.

Seeing all the vessels at anchor in White Bay, they decided to see what was happening. Their intrepid skipper-- peering intently over the rim of his glass of Bourbon high atop the flying bride-- confidently spun the wheel over, and attempted to gain entrance to the anchorage by powering over the reef. What he lacked in intelligence, he more than made up for in velocity. But-- alas!-- even using full power, they couldn't seem to get the four feet draft of their vessel over the three inch deep reef.

In any event, they clearly proved they weren't timid at the throttles, and they'd still be out there chopping up coral heads with their props if Big Jack Simmons hadn't went out and rescued them by appling a tiny bit of logic and a two horse power dinghy to the problem.

They soon joined the party on the beach, and fell into the swing of things. The skipper's wife confessed-- after tossing off a few bottles of Cruzan Rum, dancing with Limbo Dean, and chatting with beautiful Justine Callwood, "Gee, what a lucky break it was to smash into that silly reef! If it hadn't been in the way, we'd have missed the party!"

Like most parties on Jost, it ended only because the generator ran out of gas. Everybody crawled home, and the next day was canceled.

A TRUE FERRY TALE

St. Thomas, USVI-- On Tuesday night, September 24th, as the 9 p.m. St. John ferry was pulling away from the Red Hook dock, a St. Johnian women arrived slightly 'behind' schedule. She rushed down the dock, and began yelling for the ferry to stop.

Already in motion, the ferry captain kept going. The women--who was both slightly drunk and totally exasperated-- immediately dropped her pants, faced away from the ferry passengers, and bent over.

The ferry's passengers-- amused by the show-- stomped their feet and whistled. The ferry skipper-- fearing a riot-- returned to pick up the tipsy tizzy.

A tourist couple-- new to the islands-- watched the whole scene with a smile. "This is our first 'moon' light cruise," they giggled.

An Old Chartering Trick

As a journalist, I am a professional eavesdropper. I constantly listen to those around me-- especially in seedy waterfront dives where local sailors let their guard down. Many a sea tale which was only whispered across a fist-banged bar by a seaman 'hard aground on the mahogany reef'-- has appeared in these pages.

Example: a few nights ago I was at the Warehouse bar in Red Hook, killing off a few extra brain cells.

Next to me sat an Old Salt talking to an Earnest Young Kid.

The Old Salt has been chartering out of St. Thomas since before the missionaries arrived, and the Ernest Young Kid had just arrived in the islands a few days ago. He'd managed to snag command of an old trashed Out House 41 before the ink was dry on his 6-pack license-- and was think'n pretty highly of himself.

The Old Salt wasn't saying much-- concentrating instead on sucking up the Kid's liquor. The Kid was attempting, naturally, to pump the ole duffer for as much information as possible on how to play the chartering game.

"One thing I think is especially important," said the Kid expansively, "is First Impressions. It's of paramount importance to make a professional, competent impression on your guests right off the bat-- especially if you want a big tip..."

The Old Salt was muttering something about big tips, whales, and fine art of circumcision-- but the kid didn't catch it. The Kid then nonchalantly asked the Old Salt exactly how he started off a charter.

"Well, first off," said the Salt. "I beat across Pillsbury Sound lugging as much sail as I possibly can. When every one is the proper shade of green, I drop the hook in Maho Bay. I make a point to bring all my guests ashore to the beach about an hour before dusk-- and tell them I'll be right back after I throw away

10

the garbage. Then I return to the boat and take a nap."

"What about the guests," said the kid. "What about their dinner..?"

"They are dinner-- for the no-see'ums and the mosquitos," said the Old Salt. "By the time I get them back to the boat, they look like raw hamburger. The rest of the charter-- in comparison, of course-- is utter bliss to them. I never have a problem. And if they want to go to some anchorage I don't want to go to, I readily agree, saying, "Sure! Great Spot, though it can get a little buggy..."

I could tell the Kid didn't know whether he was being put-on or not. Neither did I. Only the Old Salt did.

And he wasn't telling-- not really.

Which is as it should be, I guess. We all finished up our drinks and went home happy. The Old Salt got a free drunk, I got My Story, and the young Kid learned not to trust either one of us...

Rambling Ray's Real Reef Adventure
or
How Not to Make a Splashy Entrance at
Night while Well-Lit without Running Lights
or
What Not to Do, and Who Not to Do it With!
or
How to Kill a Million Marine Orgasms..., er Organisms!

This sea story is not an easy one to tell-- impossible with a straight face-- and some of the details were a little fuzzy the next morning. Real fuzzy.

Even deciding where to begin is difficult. Did it start when Captain Ray of the 35 foot sloop "Truth Seeker" first sailed into the Back Yard Bar on St. John a few years ago? Or later-- when he attended the Virgin Island Snot Club's (VISC) "You-Gotta-Gotta- Regatta" and witnessed some of the most brutal seamanship ever exhibited this side of Hell? Perhaps it really started when he decided to donate a week-end sail to help raise funds for a vessel dismasted during that bizarre event.

Or was it Fate? Personal Destiny? Some Crazy Cosmic Consequence for a Colorful Caribbean Character?

In any event, Captain Ray took off for a week-end sail to get away from the hustle and bustle of St. John. On board were four other people-- two of which had never sailed before (or since!).

They had a nice sail up to the north entrance of Virgin Gorda Sound. "Truth Seeker" has no engine, and because of a dying breeze, they failed to make harbor before dark. Still, there was a full moon-- and besides, hadn't Captain Ray sailed her from New Zealand without a single serious mishap?

-= =-= =-= =-

Unbeknownst to Captain Ray, the cruising contingent of the

VISC was anchored just inside the reef-- off Prickly Pear island-- on their 2nd Annual "Snooze & Booze Cruz". They were in the middle of one of their disgusting food orgies-- slurping up massive amounts of Lobster, Conch, Shrimp, Grouper, and Rot Gut Rum-- and attempting to live up to their reputation of "...just a little bit too much is just enough for us..."

As usual-- when they weren't actually satiating one of their primal, base needs-- they were worried about one of their brethren-- and with good reason. One of their members who had left the USVI had never arrived in the BVI. ("VISC members can get lost in a safe deposit box," boasted one.)

Now the VISC is notorious for their... total lack of... common sense. They may be the only sailing club in the world whose motto is "What we lack in intelligence, we more than make up for in velocity!"

They know-- from hard experience-- that nothing goes right when they're in sight, so they were all very aware of the sailing vessel with the dim masthead light just outside reef.

"Do you think that's one of us," hiccuped one demented VISC member to another.

"Naw," said the fellow with a burp, "can't be. The skipper's steering too straight of a course... Probably Anita Bryant at the helm..."

-= =-= =-= =-

Now I have a confession to make, Dear Reader. I was there. With the VISC. Why?

Well-- I was chilling out from a heavy week of covering the Fisheries Conference for The Daily Snooze (A Gnat publication!)-- and lecturing the VISC about marine refrigeration. (I almost had a riot on my hand as I started my lecture. "Aw, mon, I dint know ya gonna talk 'bout dat kindda reefer," moaned a VISC member.)

Least you think it strange that I was lecturing such a group on such a serious subject, let me point out their last three

13

speakers were: Donald Crowhurst-- "Racing Ethics", D. Conner-- "Ten Days to a Slimmer Skipper", and J. Slocum-- "Sex and the Single-Hander."
Or at least that's what they claim.

-=-=-=-=-=-

Where were we, eh? Ah, yes! Captain Ray was sailing "Truth Seeker" between the reefs... nice as can be... when the full moon hid behind a slow moving cloud. "Which way," called Ray to his dual bow watch.
"Port starboard!" said one, while the other shouted "Starboard port!" and the boat went crunching up on the reef like a cement truck going through a chicken coop.
Stuck. Really. Really. Stuck.
And Captain Ray had no search light, no engine, no radio, no nutt'n! Nobody knew where he was. Nobody.

-=-=--=-=--=-=-

Just at that moment, I happened to stop kissing which ever young 'ting' that had crawled into my arms in need of immediate physical affection, and saw Ray's wallowing masthead light suddenly come to a shuddering, sickeningly stationary halt. "That's got to be one of us," somebody said disgustedly as they spit into the sand.
"What a bummer," said somebody laying in the sand. "Just when it's starting to sprinkle..."

-=-=--=-=-=-

Now-- if there's one thing the VISC has experience in-- it's helping people in trouble. Unfortunately, they never learn from their experiences. So the usual fistfights broke out over who would get which beer cooler, who swiped who's gas tank, and which deflatable dinghy to ruin this time.
Amid all the chaos, I managed to crawl into a large Zodiac

with a dangerously powerful engine-- and knocked all but two of the VISC members already in it overboard before I sped away.

My fellow rescuers-- a giant bearded beast named Jack, and a distinguished fellow named Thrasher-- seemed docile enough. (Not that I'd ever turn my back on 'em, you understand.)

-= =-= =-= =-

I had to stop the Zod quite far away from the grounded vessel so I didn't chew up our prop. I immediately recognized the boat. "Ahoy, Captain Ray! 'Truth Seeker'! Whatta you say?"

Captain Ray heard my voice across the water, and couldn't believe his double dose of bad luck. First he'd sailed his boat up on a reef, and now he realized the entire episode would be splashed across the front pages of...

"Oh, no," he moaned. "That's not CAPTAIN FATTY, is it? Not CARIBBEAN BOATING??!!"

"Yeah, Mon," I said gently as I whipped out my waterproof steno book and started scribbling away with my leak-resistant flashlite pen. "Exactly how do you spell your last name, Ray?"

If curse words were dynamite, he'd have blown himself off the reef right there.

-= =-= =-= =-

I won't bore you, Gentle Reader, with the rest of the story. Suffice to say, we managed to pry "Truth Seeker" back into deep water with the able help of Nick Trotter on his powerful vessel "Reef Sampler" and a stout anchor rode to the top of the mast.

I can still remember Captain Ray screaming, "Tell 'em to stop! They're tearing our bottom out!" as I calmly spoke into the hand-held VHF we'd brought, "Yeah, OK, you've taken the slack out of the tow line, now how 'bout pour'n some coal to her, huh?"

I can still hear that horrible sound a well-built plastic boat makes as it pulverizes a reef to smithereens.

I can still feel that immense sense of relief as "Truth Seeker" suddenly shot off the reef backwards at about ten knots...

-= =-= =-= =-

The next day, Captain Ray bought all the VISC members free drinks at the Bitter End Bar. It probably cost him more than his boat was worth.

Everyone learned an important lesson: even an excellent seaman like Ray-- who has sailed so extensively without mishap-- can get himself into trouble on a calm night... if they don't pay close attention to what they are doing. Luckily, no one was injured, and the damage to the boat was slight.

The Commodore-for-Life of the VISC was there, and made Captain Ray a 'life-time member in bad standing' of the club.

There was some discussion of whether this unfortunate, atypical incident might affect Ray's chances of winning the 1987 Blue Water Cruising Medal.

"Don't worry, Ray," said the VISC Commodore-for-Life. "We'll put in a good word for you..."

When Ray heard that, he _really_ looked panic stricken!

THE OLD MAN

I was nodding off in the Peace and Plenty Bar in Georgetown, Great Exhuma-- nursing a lukewarm Rum and Coke, and escaping from the noon-day sun-- when I first caught sight of "Old Gal" limping towards the dock. I slid off my bar stool- - slack jawed with amazement-- as she ghosted by. To say she was in terrible shape would be a vast understatement-- she looked like she'd been trashed by the Hell's Angels, and then struck by a small nuclear weapon.

Her bowsprit was sheared off, and her forestay gone. The port spreader dangled from the rig. The rail was ripped away on the starboard side, and-- as she approached-- I could see her topside planking was rudely caulked with... socks. Under the water, I could see that the bottom of her rudder had been eaten away, and its shaft badly bent.

She was the kind of vessel a bleeding Haitian sailor on an inner tube surrounded by sharks might pass by.

"What the hell happened," I asked as I took his bowline. "Did you hit a reef?"

There was only one person aboard. He was a grizzly old man, with stained yellow hair, and a thin, scratchy beard. He glared at me through the harsh glinting sun of the lower Bahamas, and opened a toothless mouth.

"A reef? A REEF!" he shouted. "Do you think that I did all this damage on a single reef? Do you think I'm crazy? Hell, no, laddie! I've hit reefs! Lotsa 'em! Why I've struck every frig'n reef between here and New York City! As a matter of principal! Why, I sail miles out of my way to crunch into one!"

There was something about his gruff bellowing that I immediately liked. Here was a man that didn't care what anyone thought. I smiled at him.

"Don't smile at me, laddie," he said. "Or I'll move into your neighborhood and make the property values plummet!"

"You're funny," I blurt out.

17

"Yeah," he said, and got serious all of a sudden. He coughed up some flem and spit it over the side. "Funny as cancer."

"You've lost some of your rudder."

"Yeah, but it was too big to begin with. Just right now. Watch my boat for a few minutes. I need to get some supplies."

He had a huge German Shepherd aboard. It went over to the sheet winches on the port side of the cockpit, lifted a leg, and peed on them.

"Nice doggy," I muttered at it.

The old man was soon back (or as they say in the islands, "Dat mon, he just go to come...") and he had a small block of ice in one hand, and a half gallon of local rum in the other. Under an arm was a carton of Camel cigarettes. "Come aboard," he said to me. "Sit a spell. Swig a little of my swill. Gam abit."

I hopped aboard "Old Gal" and the moment I glanced below from the cockpit, I realized why she had such little freeboard. The cabin was half filled with water. I couldn't even see the floorboards.

We settled in the cockpit. The old man put the block of ice at his feet, and we passed the rum bottle back and forth. I kept expecting him to go below for glasses and use some of the ice, but he never did. I watched the block shrink into nothingness under the hot, glaring, fly-buzzing tropical sun.

I took little sips, while he gave the bottle serious, let's-get-drunk-and-fast pulls. He bubbled it three times to my one.

"Got a lot of water over your floorboards," I said.

"No, laddie. You're wrong there. I used to have a lot of water over my floorboards-- until I threw my floorboards away. Now I just got a lot of water!"

"Where're you headed?"

He looked at me like I was crazy.

"Where? Same place as everyone else, I guess. Paradise. Some place where you don't have to wear hip boots to wade through the bullshit. How 'bout you."

"Yeah," I said. "I reckon I'm heading that away too."

I kept glancing below. It was the most primitive interior I've ever seen in a boat. Just a single piece of plywood for a bunk- - without cushion or pillow. The galley was a single burner camping stove, and scattered plastic milk crates served for stowage. There was nothing else, save for a three-quarters submerged hunk of rusted iron forward, that looked vaguely familiar in shape.

"I'm too old to hop freights," said the old man. "And I don't like sleep'n on steam grates. Kept falling asleep in the soupline at Sally's Army. And anyway, all the bag ladies wouldn't laugh at my jokes. So it's a sailors life fer me."

I didn't know what to say to that, so I moved the conversation back to safer ground. "Your boat needs a little work."

"Some," he said. "But not much. All she's got to do is to outlast me."

"You look healthy as a mule," I lied. He looked like he was going to keel over any second, but I wanted to cheer him up. He wasn't having any of it.

"I usually don't share my liquor with fools, son," he said. "But since ain't nobody else around, I'll make an exception in your case."

I looked away from his eyes, and bubbled the rum bottle a couple of times-- trying to catch up.

"Now doctors are supposed to be smart," he said out of the blue. "But they're about as useless as a fart in a bathtub. They told me if I stopped drink'n, and smoke'n, and sleep'n under the stars... that I might-- just might-- live a few days longer. They had a real fancy prison where they wanted to put me so that when I drooled on myself, nobody would get upset. Well, my laddie, I told them to take all their fancy-school ideas and shove them up where the sun don't shine.

"My wife died. Just like that. One minute she was telling me a juicy story about one of the neighborhood wives whor'n around, and the next minute... ain't-nobody-home. I always thought that I would be the first to go, but the Ole Bitch foxed me in the end. If there's any dying to be done, laddie, hop in first. It's a helluva lot easier."

19

I didn't say anything, and he didn't seem to mind.

"So I sold everything-- which wasn't much-- and bought "Old Gal". She ain't much, but neither am I. We're suited for each other. Both passed our prime, and creaking for the Pearly Gates."

We both stopped and watched as the dog pooped on the cabin house. It was downwind, and didn't matter.

"I got to working for a rich couple on Long Island. They were both lawyers, robbing folks using a brief case instead of a gun. Legal crooks, they were. But they took a hanker'n to me. Rich folks like to have somebody around that will call a spade a spade. It amuses 'em.

"Anyway, I did odd jobs for them, and occasionally they'd toss a few pennies at my feet. They were cheap, cheap people, like most of the rich, and I figured that if'n it cost them a nickel to take a shit, they'd vomit. But one day they surprised me.

"They gave me a powerplant. They got a new Jap job to use around the estate to power tools where there weren't no electricity, and they just gave me the old one.

"It set my mind to thinking. What's the difference between the United States and the Third World? Electricity! And here I was with a machine that you poured gasoline in one end, and out came that magic, invisible juice from the other. Well, it didn't take me long to toss that gizmo aboard, and start sailing!"

With a start, I suddenly realized what the rusted hunk of metal that was submerged below was. It was an old fashion Briggs and Stratton generator. His "powerplant".

"So I'm on my way to the islands. Gonna find me a spot that needs electricity, and set myself up as king. Might even get me one of those fat-mama woman, and see if I can get the plumbing to work again."

-= =-= =-= =-

The next day, I stopped down to help him fix up the boat--

but he brushed me aside. I think he was embarrassed about how freely he had spoken the evening before. I have a knack for getting people to talk, which is just another way of saying I know when to shut up. A week later, with a new bowsprit, forestay, and some additional rudder strapping, he was gone.

Last I heard of "Old Gal", she was working her way to the east along the south coast of Haiti. Ducking into all the coves, checking things out.

I don't know what happened. He never showed up in St. Thomas, although I had the whole Virgins alerted to keep a sharp eye out for him. I like to think that the Good Lord took him just as he was broad reaching into the harbor of his dreams. And finally gave him Paradise at last.

A Lim'n Philosopher on Jost

It was like a scene from a picture postcard. An elderly couple-- looking like they'd just fallen out from the pages of Modern Maturity magazine-- strolled down a deserted beach on the island of Jost Van Dyke in the British Virgin Islands. They were from East Greenwich, Connecticut, and were chartering for the first time in the Caribbean. He wore the latest in yachting togs, she a simple floral dress. They held hands. The Trades rustled their silver hair. The caption on the back of the postcard might read, "The Golden Years-- A Retired American Couple Vacation in Paradise."

They came upon a young West Indian fisherman dozing under a palm tree. They soon struck up a conversation.

The fisherman was relaxing after work, though it wasn't yet noon. He'd went out fishing, caught enough to feed his refrigerationless family, and returned to shore.

The tourists joked with him for being so lazy. "If you'd kept fishing, you might have caught enough fish to make it worth your time to bring them to St. Thomas and sell them to the restaurants," said the man.

The tourist man had been in the wholesale meat business many years ago, and knew of such things.

"Ya," said the fisherman, "dat true too, Mon."

"And if you'd fish a full day, five days a week, you'd probably soon have enough money to buy a real fishing boat with an inboard diesel engine, instead of having just an open outboard skiff..."

"Dat be nice," said the fisherman with a grin.

"With a real fishing boat, I'm sure you'd be able to increase you're productivity," said the tourist. "If you were frugal, you'd soon have a little nest-egg set aside for another vessel..."

"Two boat fleet," said the fisherman excitedly, clearly getting off on the story. "But how I fish two boat when I only one

22

mon?"

"You'd have to hire someone," said the tourist. "and with another man working for you-- and you taking some of their profits-- why in no time you could..."

"...retire, and lay 'round de beach all day in dey shade," finished the fisherman.

There was a long moment of silence, then the fisherman started laughing. He had a nice, clean laugh-- totally without guile.

Then the tourist couple started laughing, and everyone was grinning at everyone else.

A bottle of unlabeled rum appeared, and they passed it around like kids. Even the woman bubbled the bottle.

They soon parted company, and each returned to their own world. The fisherman dozed off under the palm tree, and the tourist couple glanced at their gold Rolex watches-- making sure they didn't miss the boat that would bring them to the plane that would return them to the rest of their lives.

BABY ABOARD!

It was a tense moment. "Don't play games," said the uniformed man with a gun as he glanced out the ports of "Carlotta". His grey gunboat lay dead in the water-- a hundred yards to windward-- its foredeck machine gun at the ready. Both vessels rolled sickeningly in the glassy ocean swell just off the north coast of South America-- within sight of the island of Trinidad. "The clearance papers issued to this vessel by Grenada clearly lists three crew members. I only count you and your wife. What happened to the other fellow?"

"In there," I repeated, pointing to the dimly lit forepeak. Then sharply, "Roma! Roma Orion! Wake up!"

Her tiny head immediately popped up amid the sailbags. Two pudgy fists rubbed her sleepy eyes. Her sun-drenched hair framed her three-year-old face. "What's up, Dad," she yawned questioningly. "My watch?"

-= =-= =-= =-

That was three years ago. Roma Orion is almost six now, and has had many sea-going adventures since. But I clearly remember that day as the Trinidadian Navy/Coast Guard boarding officer blinked in surprise at discovering such a pint-sized crew member. He marveled at her dog-eared passport, with its multitude of stamps. "Hell," he said with grudging admiration, "She's got more sea-time than I do!"

Roma Orion was six weeks old when we took her for her first sail-- a thousand mile beat dead into the teeth of the Nor'east Trades. I can still see her as an infant, sleeping peaceably in her bunk as "Carlotta" bashed her way through the ocean swells which lay between Florida and Antigua. I can still remember the smell of baby oil and talcum powder mixing with the scent of our kerosene lamps, freshly laid varnish, and the oiled oak deck beams. How the sound of Roma suckling at my wife Carolyn's breast blended into the sounds of the hull working, the sails pulling, the rig creaking.

By the age of one, Roma knew she lived on a 36 foot ketch her parents had built in Boston. That life was a giant adventure. That the love you got was equal to the love you gave. By one and a half, she could point to the bow and stern, port and starboard, fore and aft. At two, she helped us clean and maintain the boat, could tell the difference between a yawl and a schooner, and would yell "pinching!" whenever I'd inadvertently luff.

At three she could swim like a fish, regularly catch a fish as big as herself, and had begun standing her 'watches'-- regular ten minute periods where she was responsible for keeping a look-out for other vessels, monitoring the self-steering device, and keeping an eye on sail trim.

At four she began learning how to steer. "Good girl! Good Girl! Now a little more to port. Good. A little more. OK. Enough. Straighten out. Now back the other way. Starboard. Good girl! GOOD Girl..!"

At five she began the long (endless?) process of learning to sail. And as a reward for her being able to read at the second grade level, she was allowed to begin steering the outboard powered dinghy.

Needless to say, my wife and I are proud of Roma Orion. But that isn't what surprised us. We expected to be proud of her. What amazed us was how much she has changed our cruising life.

With my background, it shouldn't have.

My first memory is also of the sea. My dad is framed in the

companionway of the 52 foot Alden schooner "Elizabeth". His black bushy beard is full of lather, and there is an old fashioned razor in his hand. He's shaving while I steer. I feel a million miles tall with the helm in my tiny hands.

"Another spoke to starboard, son. Good. Steady as she goes. Now port! Meet her, son-- meet her! Good. GOOD boy!"

I too grew up aboard. My entire childhood was spent living on "Elizabeth", along with my two older sisters and my younger brother. My family eventually sold that boat when I was twelve, but I managed to purchase my own cruising boat at 15 years of age with money saved working after school for a sailmaker.

In fact, I have lived over 25 of my 35 years aboard various sailing craft. I built "Carlotta" (ten tons of blood, sweat & tears) when I was 19 years of age. And I have spent a lifetime doing what many men only dream of-- seeing what is just over the horizon. So when my wife and I married, and we decided to have a child, I certainly didn't seriously consider stopping.

For me, growing up on the schooner "Elizabeth" was like growing up in a fairytale. The world was our oyster, the boat safe harbor, the family our universe. The world was a simple and just place. People were good and true and faithful. The laws of nature were fair, if unforgiving. There was a time to joke and a time to reef, a time to soak up the sun and a time to endure the frigid north wind at the helm. A very good time.

And now I am raising my own daughter aboard, attempting to give her at least a taste of the wonderful childhood with which I was blessed.

Roma means "to wander... a Gypsy." Orion is a navigational star useful in rude, lifeboat navigation. Thus we named our child in the hopes she would travel through life with an inborn sense of direction. What more could any parent hope for?

I have no desire that Roma Orion follow in my watery footsteps. I would just as soon she marry an inland farmer as a 12 meter bowman. I don't want her to follow the sea-- but I DO want her to follow the lessons that the sea has taught her. And I pray her future husband realizes that nature is not something to tame, to beat, or to change-- but something to live with in harmony.

The sea is a great teacher-- for both parent and child.

Roma Orion has changed our cruising lives greatly-- she's made it better. We're able to see anew through her wide, questioning eyes. We're able to sense again God's grace in the wheeling flight of a laughing seagull. We're able to hear the sounds of the sea for what they really are: a lullaby.

And as a family we're able to relearn the most important lesson of all: that the world is still a true and just place, that nature is still fair, if unforgiving. And that the folks who inhabit it-- be they seamen or farmer--are still good.

Bareboat Nightmare!

On Friday, January 15, the crew of the bareboat "Accordion" suffered through one of the most gruesome nautical chartering experiences I've ever witnessed. It didn't last long. Only twenty minutes. But by the end of it, the boat looked like it had been trashed by the Hell's Angels-- wires, cables, hoses, doors, floorboards, gauges, shifters, etc., were all spewn about the boat like a bomb had went off. There was a whimpering lady in the cockpit (who probably hadn't been too keen on chartering anyway) who was ranting about 'demonic possession'. Half the crew had donned life-jackets, while most of the others appeared to be reciting the Last Rites. The boat was belching smoke, oozing oil into its bilges, and was worth considerably less than moments ago. Everyone aboard was shaking like a leaf.

Including me.

It was like something out of a weird Stephen King Novel-- sort of a nautical version of "Christine".

Here's what happened.

-==-==-==-

Just before dark, the crew of "Accordion" was setting at anchor in Cruz Bay, and watching the sun set in the west. Everything was groovy-- just like an advertisement from a chartering brochure. They were charging the batteries. Another bareboat was anchoring ahead of them. A dilapidated dinghy with a cute child, an attractive woman, and an ugly obese guy was passing by. Everything was tranquil and serene...

...and then their diesel (nobody even near the controls) revved up. And stayed revved up. High Revs. SUPER HIGH REVS! The whole boat started shaking, shaking, SHAKING!!!

And then the engine slipped into gear with an awful whining

noise, and the boat shot forward like a startled deer-- and smashed into the boat ahead of it. Glanced off. Smashed into another boat. Glanced off. Smashed into another...

Their anchor was still down, and they were churning through the anchorage smashing, crashing, and dashing...

Off course, by this time their intrepid skipper had jumped aft to the engine controls and had attempted to get the vessel under control. He attempted to throttle down. The throttle didn't work. He attempted to take the engine out of gear. The shift didn't work. He attempted to shut off the engine by pushing the kill button. The engine wouldn't shut off. It was running. It was in gear. And that was that. The hot-metal-to-hot-metal screeching it produced made rational thought difficult.

So the crew of the "Accordion" stood on the foredeck screaming in mindless horror as their vessel played 'boat-billiards' with the other craft anchored nearby.

The scene was a fiberglass repairman's wet dream!

The air was filled with the sounds of boats getting T-boned, stantions snapping, rigging ripping, stern pulpits bending, chainplates tilting, gel coats gouging, and fiberglass tearing...

...the "Accordion's" anchor was still down, so she was scribing a giant arc within the crowded anchorage-- hitting the same scared/scarred vessels again and again and again....

Needless to say, I was the unfortunate ugly fat fellow in the dinghy who just happened to be going by. I'd already spent a tough day at the beach flirting with young girls while waiting for my old lady to get off of work-- and was in no mood for getting involved in any silliness. And I pride myself on my callousness.

But those poor folks huddled on the bow of their boat looked so pathetically horrified-- even my heavily hardened heart was forced to take pity on them.

I swung my dinghy alongside, jumped aboard, grabbed the wheel, screamed, "CUT THE ANCHOR LINE..!"-- and in an instant we were flying out of the harbor away from the debris at over eight knots.

As soon as we were clear of other vessels, I gave the helm

over to the closest guy who wasn't drooling on himself, and went below to shut off the diesel.

Now I've worked on FOUR 108's a lot. Even owed a few. I like 'em, even.

And I have certainly never seen one which wanted to keep running as badly as this one. The STOP control was useless, as was the shifter and throttle. I ripped open the engine compartment, and attempted to choke off the air supply with a pillow-- but was unable to accomplish it. (Pillow stuffing swirled everywhere.) I attempted to shut off the fuel supply, but there was no shut-off at the tank or the fuel filter that I could see. I went back on deck, tore the back of the Morse engine controls off with my bare hands, and attempted to either throttle down the engine or shift it out of gear. Even removing the cables and operating them manually didn't work.

I called the charter company on the VHF, told them we were having a rough day, and asked them how to shut off their overly enthusiastic engine. They didn't seem to know.

I told them it was oozing oil, hot, stinky, and rather unpleasant-- and that I was going to shoot it with a fire extinguisher (deprive it of oxygen) if it was OK with them.

It wasn't.

I said something into the VHF I hope the FCC didn't hear.

Then I dove back into the engine room, and-- using a piece of a mahogany cabin door as a pry bar-- managed to wrench the throttle cable clean off the engine. Flipping the lever back and forth at the fuel pump didn't make the slightest difference on RPM.

At this point, I too started to believe that perhaps the engine was actually possessed by the devil!

On the other side of the engine-- starboard-- I wrenched off the cable to the hydraulic transmission. I was unable to get it into neutral-- though I did find reverse a few gut-wrenching, metal-tearing times.

By this time, I admit I was a blubbering massive mass of jello. With a body weight which matches the national debt, and an IQ which is lower than my age-- it dawned on me maybe

I shouldn't keep pretending to be a Good Samaritan.

Just attempting to crawl around an engine spinning at twice its rated RPM-- just the horrible noise!-- was driving me crazy. My brain-- never too quick since the '60's-- was nearly paralyzed with frustration. I actually-- just for an instant!-- contemplated throwing up into the air intake in a desperate, humanistic attempt at drowning the damn thing!

I finally managed to choke the beast to death-- despite my earlier failure. This time I pried off the air cowling until I had a flat round hole, then sealed it off with a thin layer of rubber held in place by a women's purse compact.

I was covered with oil, bleeding from every knuckle, covered with sweat and the stink of fear, screaming at the top of my lungs, "DIE! DIE! DIE, you mudder f....!!!" when it shut off and boat was silent.

Never has silence sounded so good.

I looked around the interior of the boat. Hot oil-- which oozed from every orifice of the melting engine-- had been whipped around by the whirling fan belts. The engine was a pathetic shamble-- with hoses, controls, wires, and pipes twisted clean off. In my haste to kill the engine, I'd yanked off various parts of the varnished wooden interior with my bare hands. While upside down, my feet had shattered a mirror, and kicked off a bulkhead lamp. The aft cabin bunk had a huge oil stain where I'd slithered across it to gain access to the engine control cables...

...and pillow stuffing still floated crazily in the air.

I ambled on deck. I must have been quite a sight. My hands were like claws. They dripped spots of blood and oil onto the deck.

The life-jacketed bareboaters shrank away from me as I approached-- as if I was a ghost. "Who is he?" whispered one of the woman to her husband. "Where did he come from?"

My wife-- scowling with disapproval-- swung along side with our dinghy to take me off. Even my six year old daughter seemed to be smirking.

We were way out into Pillsbury Sound.

31

As I attempted to slither into my dinghy without tearing their stantions off the deck-- they asked me my name.

"Fatty," I said wearily.

It is not easy for middle Americans to call somebody 'Fatty".

"Thank you, Fatty," they said, obviously struggling.

"At your service," I said with a jaunty wave of my bruised hand.

Later that evening, as my wife was bringing me yet another bottle of rot-gut, she asked, "Did you get a story out of it?"

"I better have," I hiccuped.

Chartering Pioneers

The entire USVI charter industry-- which has grown so rapidly into such an important part of our local economy-- wasn't originally masterminded by some far-sighted sailing entrepreneurs intent on making a massive amount of megabucks.

Instead, the chartering industry organically evolved from a divergent group of Caribbean sailors who were endeavoring-- not to be rich-- but to figure out a way to earn enough money to maintain their vessels so that they could sail in Paradise forever.

Some of them have done just that.

Captain Neil Lewis-- who currently owns and operates the day charter vessel "Alexander Hamilton" in Red Hook-- has been chartering continuously for over 26 years now. He still looks forward to each sail, each guest, each opportunity to display his love for these islands.

A day sail with Captain Lewis is not only enjoyable and relaxing-- it's also a delightful short history course in the evolution of the chartering industry of the Virgins. He's seen it all.

"Almost all the boats were owner-operated back then," Captain Lewis recalls. "The average age of the skippers was around 50 years-- not 26 like today. There was a great sense of camaraderie. I started out with a 26 foot boat called 'Chiquita'. Bill Beer started a few years later on 'True Love'-- Don Street was chartering back then-- of course Dyke and Inga..."

"The very first 'charter' in the USVI's," Captain Lewis explained, "wasn't planned. A fellow named Basil Symonette aboard a boat called "Sea Saga" was approached by some tourists back in the '40's, and offered money to take them sailing around St. John..."

Thus crewed chartering-- Virgins Islands style-- was born.

33

Dick Avery (who is currently off-island bringing his new boat down from the States) came to the USVI back in the '50's. He was soon chartering the 63 foot Ray Hunt designed schooner "Victoria" for $900 bucks a week-- plus $6 per day per person for food.

He quickly noted that many of his charter guests owned boats back home, and were perfectly capable of captaining vessels in the Virgins.

Why not have a few simple (bare) boats for rent, he thought.

Thus bareboating was born.

There are, according to reliable sources within the industry, nearly 600 bareboats currently for hire in the USVI's and the BVI's.

Dyke and Inga Wilmerding have been chartering for about the same amount of time. They still charter the Gallant 50 "Zulu Warrior" out of Red Hook, and are considered by many to be the 'grand' parents of crewed (not crude!) chartering in the USVI.

Their beautiful John Alden schooner "Mandoo" was a familiar sight in the Virgins in the early '60's, and they have many delightful tales to tell of "the good ole days'.

Dyke and Inga are still-- after all these years-- the quintessential chartering couple. They clearly love their work, each other, and their guests. Just being in their company is relaxing. They both exude an honest sense of peaceful, personal warmth which is impossible to fake.

Things were far more primitive and laid back when they started poking their bowsprits into the desert coves which have now became so popular.

People didn't expect as much.

Dyke looks back on those poverty-stricken days with great fondness. "Just before we sold 'Mandoo', she was leaking pretty badly," he told me a few years ago. "I'd sail her with one hand on the tiller, and one eye on the bilge. Whenever the pumps couldn't keep up with it, I'd tack into a handy cove, and have Inga take the guests around the point for snorkeling. As soon as they'd disappear from sight, I'd dive over the side and stuff cotton in the seams near the rudder post and horn-timber area. I'd get the leaks slowed down and be lounging on deck when they returned aboard none the wiser. Those were the days!"

Rudy Thompson, well-known for his racing aboard "COLD BEER" and other hot boats, was chartering out of St. Thomas long ago. One of his most famous repeat guests was John Steinbeck.

Steinbeck preferred offshore passages to gunkholing, and loved to take long night tricks at the wheel with only a bottle of whiskey for companionship. Rudy Thompson still treasures those memories, as well as the now tattered letters which passed between them.

Sometimes it seems like the world was bigger back then, and the men were too.

Don Street raised his now famous "Iolaire" from the bottom, shoveled out the mud, and had it chartering in less than a month. Try that with a modern Irwin 65!

Street's boat-- which was built in 1906 and is not exactly a gold-plater-- still occasionally charters. And each year she sails back and forth across 'the Pond' (the Atlantic ocean) a few times-- just to prove she still remembers how. She and her skipper have forgotten more sea miles than most sailors will ever know.

Fritz Seyfarth-- author of numerous books on the Caribbean-- was chartering his John Alden designed ketch "Tumbleweed" in the mid-sixties. He didn't make much money back then, but he didn't spend much either. Yuppies hadn't been hatched yet. Fritz chartered to nudists, a Burma Trail elephant driver, a French Ambassador, an ex-foreign legion waterboy, three window dressers from the Big Apple, and a few of the most obnoxious Alabamians ever born.

"My very first charter was one of those rare, 100-percent bummers," Fritz writes in his delightful book 'Tales of the Caribbean'. "By the time it was over, I was a basket case. I turned in my license, tore off my epaulets, burnt my 5000 brochures, and swore I'd never do it again."

35

"My friends talked me back to health, and I carried on. Except for a few problem weeks, I entertained some of the nicest people imaginable. Those were good years."

The late Bob Stout-- husband of Joni Stout-- was one of those special people who made the chartering industry what it is today. Back in the '70's, this writer once had the pleasure of listening to him keep a cockpit full of charter skippers laughing till the wee hours of the evening as he spoke of his 'good ole days' aboard his steel ketch "Dragon". (Dragon continues to be one of the most popular day charter boats in Red Hook.)

"Water was scarce back then," he said, "so I'd always tell my arriving guests that we were having trouble with the fresh water shower pump. I had a cut-off switch by my seat, and when I figured they'd soaped up enough, I'd shut it off. They'd complain-- and I'd tell 'em to get ready to rinse off quick just in case I managed to briefly fix it..."

Those were-- indeed-- the good ole days. The sea-going men and women who berthed the infant Charter Industry did it as much as a Labor of Love as for a livelihood. Because they persevered with their romantic dreams in such good humor-- the Virgin Islands has a healthy, vibrant, growing industry which benefits all of her peoples.

Hats off to those early USVI sailors who scratched their shaggily beards and dared to mutter aloud, "I wonder how I can make enough money to STAY?"

Weird Maydays in June

Two St. Johnian sailors-- identified only as Mike and Steve-- were recently forced to spend an entire night adrift in Pillsbury Sound when the outboard engine on their dinghy failed midway between Red Hook and Cruz Bay.

Since they'd forgotten to bring a flashlight, they had no means of attracting the attention of the numerous vessels which passed nearby. To fight off their boredom, they decided to spend their time dreaming up new ways to signal distress...

"We passed within a few hundred yards of an anchored Navy vessel," said one of them. "We attempted to send them a SOS by reflecting the faint moonbeams off the shiny bottom of a can of OFF insect repellant we just happened to have with us. Alas, the eagle-eyed fellow on anchor watch must have been looking the other way..."

"Next," said the other one, stifling a yawn, "we also just happened to have a can of shaving cream..."

"It was calm, and the shaving stuff floated well without breaking up..."

"So we made the letter 'H' in the water, then 'E', 'L', and 'P', and tossed in an exclamation point for special emphasis..."

They said the word "HELP!" kept expanding as it floated away, and seemed almost to glow in the dark. They hoped a passing jet liner, a balloonist with excellent night vision, or perhaps a CIA spy satellite might spot their message, and sent HELP!.

Unfortunately, none of the above happened. Instead, they were forced to wait until daybreak to sheepishly signal a passing vessel and ask for a tow.

Being conscientious seamen, they immediately requested the following "Notice to Mariners" be distributed around the waterfront-- "If sighted, please disregard the word "HELP!" written in large letters of shaving cream drifting in a westerly direction on the north side of St. Thomas..."

Another "You-Gotta-Gotta-Regatta" Scheduled

Despite all logic and common sense, plans are moving forth for the staging of the Second Last Annual "You Gotta Gotta Regatta" on St. John. This outrageous event, which last year culminated in the committee boat being taken over by 68 sun-burnt, rum-crazed nudists, will be again sponsored by the same group of disorganized sailors as last year.

"The group (which has been called every name in the book by others) is currently calling itself The Virgin Island Snot Club (VISC), and plans to once again assemble one of the sorriest fleets of sailing craft ever gathered together in one unfortunate place.

It claims to be the only club currently conducting 'honest' races in the Caribbean. "It's very simple," said a VISC spokesperson. "We win!"

It won't be a fast race. Many of the 'racing yachts' of the VISC haven't been off their mooring's since last year's regatta, and most are reported to have so much marine growth on their underbodies that they have to do an Environmental Impact Study for the EPA before they can go sailing. Scoffs one local yachtsman, "Those VISC boats are slower than jelly fish! Uglier, too!"

The awards-- which will be announced the week before the actual event, and will go only to VISC members-- promise to be as bizarre as last year. Once again, first place will win a Bowl (toilet), second a Cup (athletic), and so on...

As an added twist, VISC members have been actively soliciting the support of local merchants. Cid Hamling at Connections Answering Service has donated a busy signal. The Line Inn Restaurant has graciously agreed to chip in a melted ice cube, and the Fabric Mill at Mongoose Junction has pledged an empty spool of thread. "I just can't tell you how community support like this makes us feel," said one VISC member.

None of the standard racing rules will be in effect during the race. Boats will be discouraged from having any valid PHRF, MORC, or SORC racing certificates aboard. Safety gear is allowable, but frowned upon. Waterballooning and the pelting of other yachts with soft vegetables is encouraged-- though not mandatory. Tonnage, and the law of gravity apply.

The event, which traditionally starts at the entrance of Great Cruz Bay for those few who can find it, is open to "all sailing craft with a sense of humor," said one VISC member.

"The starting gun will probably go off considerably after the scheduled time of 12 noon on August 16th. Be there, or be square!!!"

You Gotta-Gotta-Regatta

It was-- quite possibly-- the most bizarre yacht race ever held. What other marine sporting event actually encourages you to throw things at your opponent? What other race allows you to ignore a mark if you are able to bomb a vessel which has already rounded it ?

Bomb? Throw things? What things?

"Waterballoons, soft vegetables, or small children," said a spokesman at the skipper's meeting. "Stomach contents may also be thrown, but only UP!"

On Sunday, August 16th, nearly 250 people from forty different boats participated in the Second Last Annual You-Gotta-Gotta Regatta-- a weird and twisted event sponsored by the infamous Virgin Islands Snot Club of St. John.

In terms of both Good Clean Fun and Bad Dirty Fun, it was a giant success.

Of course, nothing is perfect. There were a few problems. Only to be expected...

Er...

There were a few collisions. One boat lost its rig. Another vessel calmly completed the course, got the horn from the committee boat, and then promptly sailed up on a nearby beach and sank.

The skipper of the beached vessel, when questioned why his vessel was awash, thoughtfully replied, "I dunno."

The entire event was filmed on video. The footage of the start is awesome-- enough to give nightmares to even the stoutest yacht-racing nazi.

The cameraman-- filming his first (and perhaps last) Regatta-- is panning the fleet. A multitude of boats-- from 20 foot sloops to 50 ketches to 70 foot staysail schooners-- are milling around madly. The cameraman, braced firmly in the cockpit of the committee boat, suddenly focuses on one specific boat. Its closing fast. Too fast! BLAM!!! The collision knocks the camera out of his hands. You can hear him yelling obscenities. ... "S**T! Where's my %$#@ camera..?" He finally recovers it. Lifts it back up. And focuses on yet another collision. For an instant, it looks more like a war zone that a starting line.

No protests were lodged, since a VISC spokesperson at the skipper's meeting had already warned all racers that any protesting captains "would have their peepees whacked with a small hammer, and will not be allow to attend the after-race orgy.

None of the racers dared to risk it.

In true Snot Club tradition, the designated winners were announced before the race. This year's big winner was the beautiful Concordia yawl "Golondrina". She'll have her name lettered on the much coveted Snot Club Bowl-- a gold-leafed toilet bowl.

Actual winners were: Monohulls--- 1st Place: Details... 2nd Place: Sailing Solutions... 3rd Place: Larantee. Multihulls--- 1st Place: Spirit of St. Christopher... 2nd Place: Foxfire... Ferrocement Division--- 1st Place: Carlotta... Line Honors: Details...

-= =-= =-= =-

Perhaps the most impressive performance-- and the most unexpected-- was by the classic wooden ketch "Johanna"(ex-Merry Marie, ex-Sea Wolf). Recently purchased by Big Jack Simmons and his wife Elaine, this Atkin's designed, Morse built boat surprised everyone with her fast reaching and excellent speed to windward.

She came in fourth, beating thirty some other boats in her first race with her new owners. She was in the lead at the last mark, and only lost ground when she tacked out against the current instead of short tacking inshore. She'll bear watching at the upcoming Foxy's Wooden Boat Regatta on Jost Van Dyke.

Ken Betts-- who recently purchased the 30 foot sloop "Inshalla"-- claims that he didn't come in last. "There were

41

other boats behind me," he said. "I'm not sure they were racing, but...

When questioned about the VISC and its members, Betts replied, "This is my first race, but I don't think the You-Gotta-Gotta-Regatta is really a normal type yachting event. Its more like a Kinetic sculpture or a piece of crazy Performance Art...

There was a giant raft-up after the race, with 12 boats lashed together. Sailors wandered from boat-to-boat. Occasionally one would fall through an open hatch, down a companionway, or into a cockpit.

"Hey, nice of you to drop in..!"

No big deal.

The awards ceremony was bedlam. The MC of the event-- his brain obviously fried too long in the tropical sun-- handed out a multitude of prizes without apparent rhyme nor reason.

A bikini-- which was MIA during last years event-- was one of the prizes. Its former owner hid her face and turned bright beet red as it was given away.

Later in the evening, one amorous couple waded off the beach until they were up to their necks in water, and then... snuggled. A passing stranger was heard to remark, "I guess whales aren't the only mammals that do it in the water..."

There were six picnic tables on the beach, and two giant grills going continuously all evening. One poor fellow put on six steaks, came back a few minutes later, and they were long gone. This reporter put on 10 pieces of chicken, went to fetch a beer or two, then returned to an empty grill.

"What the hell happened to my chicken," I bellowed.

"I ate it," said a smiling fellow. Since it was the same fellow who'd lost his steaks, I couldn't get mad. Instead, I stole a few unguarded beef kebabs...

During the party, the Snot Bowl was passed, and a collection was taken for the vessel which had lost its rig. Within moments, $350 was raised, and VISC members have already begun discussing 'ways and means' of raising more funds to assist in getting the vessel ship-shape as soon as possible.

42

"Hey," said one beery & bleary eyed VISC member, "we could have a gigantic party, and..."

On the following morning, as dawn broke over the harbor, I walked down the beach. The sunken boat was still hard on the sand, with her skipper sleeping on a bit of dry deck on the high side. He woke up as I approached.

His eyes were redder than a port running light, and I was worried he might bleed to death.

It was obvious he was a life-time VISC member.

"Well," he said philosophically, "We lost one boat's rig, and we sunk another. I guess it just goes to prove that this club's S'not for everyone!"

The Back Yard Bar

The Back Yard Bar on St. John is an institution-- or at least that's where much of its staff and patrons appear to have been released from. This isn't a Fern Bar, or a Singles Bar, or a Tourist Bar; this isn't a place to network, social climb, or impress the guy next to you.

Instead, its a place to Drink. Party. Have fun. Talk. Shout. Fall in Love. Rant against the World. Play darts. Feed Mosquitos. And hug the person next to you-- regardless of race, creed, color, gender, or political affiliation.

In short: the Back Yard is the perfect place for Colorful Caribbean Characters, Wonderful Waterfront Wackos-- and, yes!, even Lush Tropical Vegetables.

It is filled with sailors, of course.

Doug Sica manages the joint, and often tends bar. He's a bartender's bartender, and has a million jokes ever ready-- each more disgusting than the last. Sometimes he wears a bow tie, and actually manages not to look too silly in it. Occasionally a woman's frilly garter belt is clamped on his upper sleeve. He sometimes looks like he fell out of an old cheap Tropical Western.

Doug knows more about a lot of people than he wants to. He's friend, confidant, and father confessor to half the people on the island. He's often hunched across the bar, earnest talking to a customer-- eyes darting everywhere for a refill signal-- listening to a Life Story.

Doug seems to realize that people's Life Stories are important to them.

Doug sees it all, hears it all, tastes and smells it all-- but like any good bartender, nothing is ever repeated, revealed, exposed, or ridiculed.

He's not the only employee, of course. There's Mean Jean the Dancing Machine, Lovango Tom, Lynnie the Singer, Doug the Cook, Arlene the Masseuse, Mark from Coral Bay, Angela, and some special evenings Miss Maggie shows up and cooks the best damn conch fritters in the Caribbean.

But of course what makes the Back Yard the Back Yard is its strangely kinetic mix of customers.

It's home to the infamous Monkey Crew-- that weird and twisted group of yachting Nazis who make up one of the most colorful yacht racing teams ever to disgrace an island. Sylvie DeFrog-- better known as the Pirate Queen-- has been known to bite patrons shirts off. Tumbling Tom occasionally manages not to fall off his stool. Scooter Mejia scoots by with his dog Turbo Stinky Sachmo in tow. Papa Davis, Bernie, Mizzen Man Kevin, and Curt the Carpenter occasionally stop by to wet their whistle.

The music wails, darts are thrown, the toilet is hot-seated, the ice machine hums, tips are thrown through the air, the cooler doors are a blur, the phone rings off the hook, people disappear heavenward, the cash register clangs; everyone is shouting, laughing, giggling, whispering, suggesting, begging, demanding, explaining...

...and it's just another night at the Back Yard.

Occasionally a tourist drifts into the madness. They seem nervous at first. But the mood soon infects them. Their hips-- normally so frozen-- get to swaying in time to the music. Somebody they have never seen before buys them a drink. Conversations ranging from necrophilia to health foods to mainsail trim swirl through the air. Jokes ("What is the difference between Cruz Bay and Rock Hudson? Well, one is a ferry terminal, and the other was a...") jostle each other for attention. There's a strange feeling of exuberance in the air. Tourists only on the island for a few days have been overheard pretending to be locals, "Yeah, Mon! I tink I'll get some ting to drink at de Yard."

Many of the construction workers who gather after a hard, long day in the hot sun, just say, "I'll be in my office."

Amid all the noise and music and shouting, it is easy to overlook the simple fact of what really makes the place so special. People.

On both sides of the bar, you couldn't get better.

The Fox of Jost Van Dyke

It's no wonder the Virgin Islands are the world's most popular chartering destination. The weather is usually perfect, the sea calm, and the islands-- like green emeralds spewn upon a turquoise sea-- are exquisite. What is amazing, however, is how many people charter in the Virgins year after year after year. When questioned, many of these repeat visitors point to the same little island and the same unique man as the reason for their return. "We came back to sail to Jost Van Dyke again, and see Foxy."

Foxy Callwood is a living legend, a real-life Caribbean myth, a wonderful-waterfront-wacko. He's one of the few native West Indian gentleman whose fame has spread far afield of his small palm-fronded world. You can mention Foxy's name in almost any port on the planet-- in the sleazy sailor's bars of the Azores, the hushed rooms of the New York Yacht Club, or the crowded dinghy dock of a Brazilian whorehouse-- just mention the Fox, and you'll soon be swapping sea stories about the Virgin Islands with a new friend.

Foxy is famous, and deservedly so. The question is: exactly what is Foxy famous for? For owning an island beach bar? For billing himself as the 'laziest man in the world'? For being the world's most laid-back stand-up comedian? For singing for his supper? For having the widest smile?

The answer is not easy. The answer is as varied as his many friends.

"Foxy is a master story-teller," says Lenora Stanciauskas who recently visited the island of Jost aboard a 36 foot ketch from Dutch Sint Maarten. "He tells of large truths in small, simple ways. Each of his tales are multi-faceted jewels, with many levels. He captivates you with his island yarns, until you're hanging on his every word. He's what so many performers wish to be; and so few are. He's spell binding!"

Another visitor doesn't even mention Foxy the Storyteller.

"I love his music," says Lawrence Best as he relaxes in the cockpit of a 52 foot blue ketch which charters out of St. Thomas. "Sure, his songs are funny and they make me laugh-- but they also make me think. Foxy has a unique talent to delight and disturb at the same time. On one level, they're just simple little tunes; on another, they're the stories of universal human folly."

Other guests on the island ignore Foxy's singing and story telling abilities, and concentrate on his business.

"Foxy's Beach Bar has a sand floor, a leaky roof, and not much else," says Captain Mark Rabinowitz of the popular 65 foot charter vessel 'Endless Summer II'. "In spite of that-- or possibly because of it-- it's the site of many of the best parties in the Caribbean. I bring most of my charter guests to Jost, and a visit to Foxy's is the highlight of many of their vacations."

Patrick McGee, off the British racing sloop "Silly McGee", has another viewpoint entirely. "Foxy is not just another 'Turd' World philosopher. He's a Caribbean entertainer in the finest tradition. He doesn't ask for respect, his mere presence demands it. He is blessed with a huge talent, and is driven to share it. He was born to make people smile!"

The island of Jost Van Dyke-- whose population is barely a hundred West Indian souls-- is only a few hours sail from Tortola, St. Thomas, or St. John. Yet it is a "million miles from reality". There was a clock on the island once, but it broke. There is no electricity, no post office, no phone booth, no policeman, and no gift shop. The biggest local news last year? One of the goats got pregnant...

The island is solely dependent on passing cruising and charter vessels for its income. Nowhere in the Caribbean is the waterborne traveler welcomed more wholeheartedly. Foxy sponsors numerous special events each year to lure vacationers to Jost. His annual Wooden Boat Regatta is one of the most popular events in the Virgins, and his traditional New Year's Eve Party is a world class blow-out not to be missed. In January 1988, he'll be having his 20th anniversary in business, and already the locals are hatching plans to make it the party of the decade.

But just why Foxy's Bar is so very special is difficult to define. There's Foxy himself, wrapped in an aura of peace and tranquility so thick you could slice it with a dull rigging knife. There's his lovely teenage daughter Justine who tends bar and shoos away the island children who like to skylark 'tween the bar stools. And there's Foxy's five year old son Christian who plays amid the bar's patrons in the largest sandbox in the Caribbean.

And of course there is Tessa-- Foxy's beautiful wife of almost 20 years. She is from Australia. Her fair cheeks blush bright red as Foxy sings a song about his sailing half way 'round the world in an old schooner to woo her. As a couple, they are as different as day and night-- he the outgoing ebony entertainer, she the private wife/mother. "I didn't even know where the British Virgin Islands were until Foxy smiled at me," she shyly admits.

There's a comfortable, "old shoe" feeling about the bar. Locals stop by for a beer. Somebody shows off a fish they just caught: another holds up a giant lobster on its way to a boiling pot. Foxy sings his songs-- often creating epic tunes off the top of his head-- as the seagulls wheel and cackle in the sky above and the fish dart and dash in the sea below. Time seems to stand still. Nothing seems to matter, save Foxy's voice, this moment, the smell of this priceless tropical air.

Each day, boats from around the world gather in Great Harbour. In the late afternoon, everyone rows ashore. To taste a little sanity on a far away island. To live a few golden moments without pretense. To relax.

But exactly who-- and what-- is Foxy? How does he weave his magic?

No one seems quite sure; yet everyone wants to discover his secret. And thus, many lucky sailors return year after year after year..."to sail to Jost Van Dyke again, and see Foxy."

Tit for Tat in the BVI

"The growing number of woman yacht racers participating in international competition is astounding," said a well-known yachtsman at the BVI Spring Regatta. "They're already making waves in this normally ultra-conservative sport. Not only are they avid-- even rabid-- competitors, but they've proven themselves to be aggressively imaginative when it comes to dreaming up new twists to the old rules..."

Some of their tactics are questionable, though.

"We were within inches of one of the boats with a large female crew as we both approached a mark." said one of their competitors. "Both vessels were reaching fast-- readying for the next tack. The tension was thick. Everybody on both boats was concentrating to the max. It was then that they did it to us..."

Exactly what did the females do that caused their competitors to totally lose their concentration, allow boat speed to slip, and completely halted their preparations for the next tack? Exactly what surprise tactic did these tricky Ladies devise to distract their competition?

"There was a group of them riding the windward rail," said the fellow. "One minute they were all grim-faced racers, and the next-- they were topless!"

"The effect on us was almost instantaneous," the fellow continued wistfully. "Our jaws dropped along with our hull speed. By the time we realized we were being deliberately distracted, the mark flew by and we were late in rounding."

There was some discussion on the "out-foxed" vessel if the tactic were legal. They decided it was, since any racer could do it, though most men wouldn't--admittedly!-- create such a stunning effect. They decided that filing an official protest would certainly make them the laughing stock of the Caribbean.

"Anyway," said our informant. "The vision was worth dropping a place!"

How to Spot A Maxi Racer

The docks of St. Thomas are currently awash with internationally famous Maxi Yacht racers. They are everywhere-- and can even be seen attempting to blend in with normal people. Needless to say, they're rarely successful. Maxi racers don't look like ordinary folks for the simple reason they are not ordinary folks.

Spotting them is easy. They almost always have pink & green zinc oxide smeared wildly on their lower lips. Each one has certain mandatory Maxi equipment-- a Gold Rolex watch big enough to require its own lifejacket, a pair of Vuarnet sunglasses worth more then Ethiopia, and a cute pair of standard issue USYRU underwear--the ones decorated with little day-glo pictures of "Stars and Stripes".

There are other subtle signs. When they see yet another stacked blonde strolling down the dock towards them, they grimace manfully, like... 'not another one!' Many of them have their vessel's name and IOR rating tattooed on their... arm-- others think that's going a bit too far.

They rarely turn their backs on a camera-- usually offering their best profile to the ever present photographers. Their topsider's are never new-- yet don't have holes in their soles. (Do they pay somebody to wear them for a few days?) They dress in super-baggy sailing shorts-- shorts so huge you'd swear they're being illegally used to increase their unmeasured downwind sail area...

Their color sense is... extraordinary, to say the least. Groups of Maxi racers strolling down a dock have been known to induce LSD flashbacks in innocent aging hippie sailors. These racers love to mix pink deck shoes with bright chartreuse-hued paisley shorts-- and then finish off their colorful outfits with a fuchsia T-shirt adorned with diamond-studded red lettering which calmly states... "Pee to Lee!"

These guys couldn't sneak into the library at Gallaudet

University...

These aren't the idle rich. These aren't the bored rich. These aren't the filthy rich.

Just the opposite! These are the clean-cut, actively interesting rich.

It is often possible-- even easy!-- to tell which crew positions a Maxi racer fills. Take your sheet trimmers, for instance. Their age, biceps, and IQ are usually pretty close. These are the guys with no necks leading up to their brain stalks-- if they stand up during a jibe, the boom says 'boom' and breaks.

The Maxi yacht owners themselves are easy to spot. They're the older guys surrounded by sailor makers, designers, and journalists. They are usually attended by a masseur who is massaging the cramps out of their right hand-- an occupational hazard of anyone forced to sign so many checks every day.

The foredeck skippers (sometimes referred to as foreskin apes-- though certainly never to their faces) are the crew men who are in charge of actually hoisting sails up and down. All the Maxi boats have large foredeck hatches to accommodate these fella's heads should they ever be so lucky as to set the chute three times in a row without dropping it in the water.

The fella handing up the sails from down below is called the 'sewer man'-- a descriptive term which needs no elaboration. Now you know why Maxi racers often toss each other in the water after a race-- and work so hard to make sure they never end up downwind of a competitor!

Of course, the sailmakers are the fellows wandering around the docks totally blissed out-- their eyes spinning dollar signs like an over-revving slot-machine. If their products don't fail, they get to convince the owners their sails were built too heavy and too strong to be competitive-- while if they do blow out, they get to make new ones anyway!

Of course, the only sure way to tell if a person is a Maxi racer is to check to see if he's surrounded by a massive mob of marauding marine media vultures such as myself. Compared to us journalists, even the most reality-prone Maxi racer can easily convince himself he's truly one of the Beautiful People.

51

Yacht racing is a curious sport-- a bunch of grown men racing against each other in the highest-tech of stone-aged craft, while surrounded be a group of journalists ever hopeful of getting a shot of Dennis Conner tossing his cookies into Long Bay for the cover of YEECHTING...

Momo the Magnificent Meets Klaus

My friend David Jansen-- known affectionately throughout the New England scientific community as Momo the Magnificent-- is a typical astrophysicist. By that, I mean he's one of those nerdy guys who can tell you the exact location of a Black Hole-- and yet can't find his own car keys. To say that his "head is in the clouds" is to put it mildly. He even looks the part-- wild hair, wispy beard, pasty skin, Coke-bottle glasses, baggy pants, mismatched socks...

Since gazing at stars doesn't pay very well, Momo owns a laundromat in Western Massachusetts. His diploma is on the wall. The laundromat is called (rather aptly, I think) Astro-Wash...

Got the picture? Momo's kindda weird.

(How do I get off on these strange tangents?)

Anyway, Momo's Big-Dream-in-Life was to make an ocean passage. Why he wanted to make an ocean passage I didn't know-- and in hindsight it certainly appears I should have asked-- but I didn't.

Before Momo went to sea with me on "Carlotta", he'd never even seen a sailboat. He certainly hadn't ever been on one.

He was an atheist, too.

Now, I'm sorry to report, he's been 'born again'. And the chance he'll ever sail anywhere with anyone for any reason is rather slim. Here's why...

Momo flew into Nassua in mid-October to help me sail "Carlotta" to St. Thomas. The 1,000 mile trip was supposed to take a week. It was supposed to be uneventful.

It wasn't.

Momo brought with him a ton of unrolled quarters, some clean clothes, and a duffle bag filled with books on Quarks in Space and Laundry Management. We set sail the next day.

The forty mile passage to Highborne Cay was a classic-- and a mild taste of what to expect. We had 30 knots of wind dead on the nose, a teeth-rattling chop, and unmarked reefs sliding by on each side...

Momo immediately started vomiting. Whether he vomited from motion sickness or just plain fear was hard to say-- but it was quickly apparent Momo was a World Class Puker. For the next three weeks, he puked as regular as a metronome...

The diesel soon overheated, and became useless. We blew the tack out of the genoa. The electric autopilot fried it's brain. The Loran packed-up. The sink drain clogged. The staysail block exploded...

...lotsa other stuff screwed up-- too much to list. It was like "Carlotta" was attempting to self-destruct.

In essence, it was about normal for the beginning of an ocean passage-- at least for me.

By the time we got to Highborne, Momo was a mess. "I quit!" he said.

Without even stopping to change his stomach-speckled T-shirt, he rushed ashore waving a billfold bristling with credit cards. He howled into the startled faces of the laid-back Bahamians. "Where's the airport? I want to rent a car! Point me at a telephone..."

I let him blow off steam-- knowing his only way off the island was exactly the same way poor Momo had arrived.

He was practically weeping as I led him back aboard "Carlotta". Once below, I did what I had to do-- I lied to him till I was blue in the face.

"It will get better," I promised. "See, today we were on the Banks-- that's why it was so rough! Tomorrow we'll be in deep water, and it will be a piece of cake..."

The next day, we left at dawn. Momo threw-up as he hauled in the anchor. The wind arose with the chain-- 25 knots, ESE, dead on the nose again. "Carlotta" began doing a drunken imitation of a horrible Michael Jackson dance. Momo, already suffering from dehydration, started to openly cry-- and lost still more precious bodily fluids. We sailed on...

All that day, all night, and all the next day. "Are we in St. Thomas yet," Momo asked excitedly as we sighted land. It was difficult to inform him that we had made exactly 49 miles to the good...

We anchored in Little San Salvador, a small deserted island. Momo was too weak to go ashore. I offered to make him a hard-boiled egg. He turned several interesting shades of green at the offer, and rushed to the head. I was forced to eat dinner listening to my Sony Walkman to blanket out the sounds of his retching...

Thus it went. Until San Salvador...

"You'll love San Salvador, Momo," I told him. "There's a big dive operation on the island, with a wonderful restaurant. A Bar filled with sex-starved woman..."

"Does it have an airport," he asked pitifully. "Ferry service? A Mail Boat..?"

I could tell I had a serious problem. It was obvious Momo was thinking of jumping ship. I don't like quitters, and I certainly didn't relish the idea of single-handing "Carlotta" across an ocean without company...

Still, I had to stop in San Salvador for water and fuel...

"No airport," I lied. Momo seemed to accept the news fatalistically. The fact that it had a dive operation and the guests must arrive and depart somehow seemed to escape him. It appeared his brain was in as bad as shape as his stomach...

As it turned out, the dive operation was shut down, and the island was a near ghost town. I took Momo ashore for some R&R, and he wrapped his arms around the first palm tree that he saw, and said, "God, it was hell out there! Never again! NEVER, EVER AGAIN!"

There was a single bar open on the island. I bought Momo a beer. Then another. Then a few more. He woke up the next day with an incredible hang-over, far out to sea.

He came out on deck foaming at the mouth, and actually attempted to bite me!

After he got over the initial shock and vented his anger by cursing me and my mother, he asked, "How much water are we in? What's the depth?"

"Oh," I said off-handedly, "about 25,000 feet."

He rushed to the loo'ard rail and fed the fishes.

"That's the last time I'm taking you bar-hopping," I said gayly.

We soon settled into the routine of ocean passage making. Two hours on watch, two hours off. Endless. It felt like we were in a time warp. Momo described it as absolute boredom, interspersed with moments of stark terror, bound together by utter discomfort...

Close enuff.

Two days out, the raw water pump on the diesel blew a seal, and we lost the engine. All that evening, the next day, and the following evening, we labored in shifts to fix it. Tools everywhere, parts rolling around, gaskets falling into the bilge. The cabin was constantly filled with the stench of diesel fuel and lube oil. Throughout it all, we were smashing, crashing, bashing against the trades.

Thirty degrees of heel.

All hatches dogged down.

Finally, we got the diesel to run.

"Hooray," I shouted as I happily wiped Momo's vomit off the tools. "We're in business again!"

Momo looked at me with dull eyes. "How much longer to St. Thomas," he asked.

"Well," I said, attempting to break it to him gently. "We're heading NE, getting a lot of Easting done, but not really getting all that much closer to where... I'd say that in the last four days we've got... oh... we've done... we've made about a hundred miles to the good..."

"Oh, my God," Momo whimpered. "I wanna DIE!"

Two days went by. We were closer to Bermuda than St. Thomas. Much closer...

One day, while in the middle of my standard meal of hard boiled eggs, salt, and beer, the bilge alarm went off. I flipped on the electric pump and sucked the bilge dry. The alarm went off again within 20 seconds. We were taking on a huge amount of water extremely fast.

It was rapidly becoming one of those sink or swim problems.

...I quickly determined that-- somehow or other-- the bilge pump was syphoning back into the boat. I immediately decided to attempt to crimp the hose. I knew this would knock out the bilge pump-- but at least I'd stem the flow...

Unfortunately, while attempting this simple task, I twisted off the 2 inch cockpit scupper drain hose-- and so had a TWO inch stream of water pouring into the boat, and NO ELECTRIC PUMP!!!

...the bilge alarm was wailing, I was upside down in the bilge with only my toes showing, when Momo came up from his bunk... "What's happening," he shouted, the panic plain in his voice.

"We're sinking," I responded in my calmest, most casual tones.

"Great!" Momo shouted amid heaves. "Super! I love Yachting! This is FUN! This is PLEASURE BOATING! Thank God, I came along..."

He was laughing a scary, out-of-control laugh. "Incidently," he giggled. "if we ever get to shore-- I'm going to KILL YOU!"

Needless to say, I managed to stop the leak before we sank...

I thought-- surely!-- that little episode would be the low point of the passage... but, as usual, I was wrong.

The next day, I noticed an abnormally large cross swell running. In the dozens of transits I've made between Florida and the Virgins, I'd never seen anything like it. I flicked on the radio and got the news.

It was bad news, of course. It came over the High Seas Operator. "Hurricane Klaus. Winds 70+ knots. Location; Between St. Thomas and San Juan. Heading north. Forward speed of ten knots..."

We were, of course, due north of San Juan. It was headed right for us... and, it was at this point that Momo became so very religious...

We started monitoring the radios, listening to vessels sinking, dismasted, or just plain gone. It was rather disheartening. The worse part was the waiting-- knowing it was going to come and

57

get you...

"I can't believe this!" Momo ranted as he stomped around the boat. "This is the '80s, fer Christ sakes! People aren't suppose to drown in hurricanes anymore!"

...by this point the "Carlotta" had been buttoned up for a solid week. Her interior reeked of sweat, mildew, diesel oil, and fear. Not a pleasant place. We felt trapped, doomed, dammed, and... very unlucky. I re-read all my books which said I was safe from Hurricanes after November 1st...(this was the 10th) and wondered, "Why me, Lord?"

For three days and three nights we ran before it, showing only our storm jib. We were lucky-- the wind never got much over 50 knots. It was the seas which scared me. The breaking waves-- well over 20 feet high-- were awesome.

We broke the mainsail gooseneck, pulled out the port cockpit combing, and broke a few blocks, Belowdecks was a disaster area: a sugar bowl shattered on the galley sole at the same moment a jar of rancid butter dashed itself to pieces. The entire floor became slicker than a skating rink...

"Carlotta" kept burying her knotmeter (10 knots) as we slid down the backs of the seas...

Well, we made it. We came screaming into St. Thomas at midnight-- with all the navigational and channel lights out. Just as we were entering, we lost all shipboard power-- no running lights, compass light, log, fathometer, etc...

Momo tossed over the anchor and his lunch for the last time. We were safe.

The next day, as dawn broke over the harbour of Charlotte Amalie, we couldn't believe our eyes. Within hailing distance of "Carlotta" were twelve wrecks. Thirty-five boats were lost on St. Thomas alone, with many more sinking on the other near-by islands...

Hurricane Klaus had been a real killer...

Momo left immediately-- if not sooner. I guess he didn't enjoy it. That was a few years ago, and he still refuses to return my calls. His wife claims he hasn't bathed since his ordeal, still awakes from nightmares screaming, "It can't be my watch already!", and continues to barf each time he sees a picture of a seascape...

Rumor has it that they are looking into buying some farm property, and plan on moving to the Midwest...

The Bountiful Sea and TV

Once upon a time, while crossing Pillsbury Sound in a dinghy, a young couple spotted a half submerged cardboard carton. They stopped, and picked it up. Inside-- gushing saltwater from every orifice-- was a brand new portable 12 volt TV.

"I wonder how long its been floating," said the wife.

"I don't know," said the husband. "What a shame!"

The couple left the TV kicking around the bottom of their dinghy (they lived on a small island near St. John.) during a particularly rainy week. It got repeatedly wet. They planned on throwing it away on St. John, but it somehow got off-loaded on their island. They left it outside on the back porch for a couple of months.

One day the husband got so bored with Life in Paradise that he went outside and hooked the TV to a battery.

Of course, the TV worked perfectly. Well, almost perfectly. The speaker made everything sound like it was underwater, and the picture was a tad wavy.

They turned it on, and watched the news.

They shut it off-- and stared at it for awhile.

Then the wife got up, picked up the TV, went outside, and threw it back into the sea.

Neither of them ever mentioned it again. Many of their friends marveled at their wisdom.

Sailing to Nowhere

As I wait for the West Indian school bus to arrive, I wonder if I've forgotten any important detail concerning our upcoming cruise. It's not that we're about to sail around Cape Horn in the dead of winter, but still, a boat must be fully prepared to go to sea-- even for a gentle sail.

Chickens scatter as the bus comes rattling into "downtown" Cruz Bay, St. John, USVI. Aboard is my five-year-old daughter Roma Orion-- a smiling white face in a sea of black. "We still going?" she immediately asks.

"Yeah," I say. "All loaded up except for our Precious Cargo."

She smiles shyly, embarrassed by my speaking to her with such intimacy in front of her school chums. "Don't be so silly, Captain Daddy-O," she says sternly. Then her eyes brighten. "Last one to the dinghy is a rotten egg!"

Roma and I row out into Great Cruz Bay where our 36 foot "Carlotta" has been nuzzling her mooring for almost a year. "Ahoy," my wife Carolyn says as Roma scampers aboard. "What did you do in school today?"

I listen to them chatter as I clap the main halyard shackle onto the dinghy bridle, and hoist the dinghy aboard.

We leave at dawn, heading south, beam reaching in the Nor'east Trades. "Carlotta" chuckles along at a stately six knots. Occasionally her bow slaps aside some spray, and rainbows dance among the droplets. I hold her battered tiller in one hand: a chipped cup of hot chicory coffee in the other. The island of St. John turns from lush green to increasing paler shades of grey, and shrinks astern.

I don't bother with the self-steering, preferring instead to take "Carlotta's" pulse through the varnished wooden stick in my hands. The hairs on my head feel the wind, my eyes follow the gentle curves of the sails, while my buttocks feel the boat humming along. God has given me all the sailing instruments I'll ever need.

I notice the foot of the mainsail could use more outhaul tension. The genoa sheet lead could come aft a few more inches. I could fly my multicolored mizzen staysail with good effect. But I'll do none of these things. I'm not out here to go fast, or to prove myself. The sea will work her magic regardless.

By lunch time, the island of St. Croix is sliding by to starboard. It looks richly inviting-- a lush tropical promise. In the cockpit, we eat cheese, grapes, and crusty dark bread. We talk of stopping-- imagine strolling down pristine beaches, slipping into the rain forest, diving silently amid teeming reefs. But it's all idle chatter. We are on a different quest, and we keep heading south into open, empty water.

I'm just finishing hooking up the Aries self-steering gear-- mid afternoon-- when Roma asks me once again. "Now, Dad? It's not rough. Please?"

"OK," I say. "Ask mom to bring your harness."

We gather forward of the mainmast. I make sure Roma's life jacket is securely fastened. I make even more sure the line to her safety harness is made fast. Then Roma and I creep out onto "Carlotta's" bowsprit.

We grab each other's wrists, and lock on. "Ready," I ask. Roma nods her head.

"YIPPPPEEEE!!!" Roma screams as I snatch her off the sprit and dangle her over the water. The bow dips, and she is smothered in the white froth of the sea. As it rears up, she's suddenly clear of the water-- soaring over the crests. Flying fish scatter. Her yelping, joyous cries of delight are almost continuous.

After a while, my arms turn to lead, and I haul Roma back aboard. Dripping like a seal upon the foredeck, she sticks out her lower lip for her pouty face. "Don't stop," she begs. "Only a few more minutes!"

We eat dinner in the cockpit. We watch the sun set to the west. The sea is blood red, the sky orange/pink/green/yellow. It's a gaudy, garish display-- as though nature is shamelessly showing off.

The sun dies quick this far south. A fat moon plays peek-a-boo through some high altitude clouds. Stars wink.

We sing songs. Roma can't carry a tune in a bucket. Carolyn's voice is high and sweet and pure. Mine is low and rough and loud. We belt 'em out: "Summertime" "That Ole' Man River" "On Moonlight Bay" "Sweet Molly Malone" Nobody claps, but nobody boos either.

Roma falls asleep in the middle of "When I'm Sixty-Four", and Carolyn lugs her below. The Sandman claims them both.

At midnight, Carolyn returns topsides, and we change watches.

I awake at dawn to the smell of bacon frying, the sound of water kissing the hull, the feeling of the boat softly reeling off the effortless miles. The exuberance of the sun startles me. I blink my way to the dinette table. My girls are already eating.

After breakfast I look at the chart. "We're at the half way mark," I say to Carolyn. "Time to flop her over on the other tack."

Out in the cockpit, we prepare to come about. Our sheet leads are checked, winch handles readied, lines uncleated. "Helm's alee!"

"Carlotta" turns majestically to port. She shudders as the first ocean swell hits her squarely. She slows, but her 24,000 pounds of momentum carry her through. For a few moments we're "asses and elbows" as the jib and staysail gets sheeted home. Then all is quiet. The boat bears off, heels sharply.

Of the million and one things stored below, one is not properly stowed. I hear a crash-- the sound of something breaking-- and start to get angry. Then I stop. "Probably didn't need it anyhow," I say to Carolyn. She smiles.

The rest of the trip is unremarkable. By the second day, most conversation ceases. Words seemed clumsy held against the backdrop of Mother Ocean. A lot of talk is just babble spewn in defense of loneliness, and here in the middle of nowhere, surrounded by nothing, on the way to meet no one, we certainly aren't lonely.

Roma naps and reads and helps sail the boat. The entire

forepeak became a sea of toys. When she get too 'antsy', we give her the Walkman and two new Walt Disney tapes.

The trip could be better. We never get "Carlotta" up to hull speed. No school of Dolphins dances for us. Carolyn doesn't find the glass fishing ball she's been in search of for the last 20,000 ocean miles.

And although I manage-- once again-- to sail toward the horizon, I never manage to reach it. And I am-- after a life time spent at sea-- no further along in that quest than when I started.

The island that was our destination appears over our bows at midnight. Its lights flicker like a jewel upon black velvet. The mountain peaks lie jagged against the night sky. A white line of beaches encircles its frothing waist. Each time we glanced up, some cosmic artist has added a few deft brush strokes of definition.

Just before dawn, we are off our intended harbor. It's approach presents no problem, but following our long standing rule of never entering any harbor in the dark, we wait for the first streaks of dawn's promise.

I coil the sheets, drape the sail covers, and square away things on deck. Carolyn putters in the galley. We turn on the radio for the first time in days.

Carolyn and I were tired but not sleepy. Roma has slept without interruption since dusk. "Time to wake up Precious Cargo," I say.

Two hours later, I take Roma back to the bus stop where I'd met her on Friday. Everything seems brighter, as if the earth has been scrubbed clean. Three days ago seems a long time.

"I went sailing," Roma proudly tells her classmates.

"Where didya sail to," asks a smiling West Indian boy missing two front teeth.

"Where?" Roma seems puzzled for an instant, but her frown is soon replaced with a smile. "Why, we sailed to nowhere-- and back!"

American Paradise Publishing is a company devoted to publishing books written *by* Virgin Islanders, *about* Virgin Islanders and *for* Virgin Islanders. Our address: POB 37, St. John, VI 00831 Call (809) 776-8346 or 693-8876 or 776-6922.

ORDER FORM

Chasing the Horizon by Cap'n Fatty Goodlander (4th Printing)
ISBN # 09631060-1-5   Price: $10.00 plus $2.00 S/H

'The Life and Times of a Modern Caribbean Sea Gyspsy'

Seadogs, Clowns, and Gypsies by Cap'n Fatty Goodlander
ISBN # 09631060-2-3   Price: $7.00 plus $2.00 S/H

'Twenty Modern Sea Stories about Colorful Caribbean Characters'

St. John People edited by Cap'n Fatty Goodlander
ISBN # 09631060-5-8   Price: $20.00 plus $2.00 S/H

'A Dozen St. John Writers Profile Twenty Residents'

Sportfishing in the Virgin Islands by Carol Bareuther
ISBN # 09631060-3-1   Price: $10.00 plus $2.00 S/H

'Everything You Need to Know...'

A Taste of the Virgin Islands by Carol Bareuther
ISBN # 09631060-6-6   Price: $16.00 plus $2.00 S/H

'A Cookbook as Diverse, Rich, and Tasty as the Food it Celebrates'

Foxy and Jost by Peter Farrell
ISBN # 09631060-4-X   Price: $12.00 plus $2.00 S/H

'A Man and His Island'

Order Form for American Paradise Publishing

Please send me _____ copies of **SEADOGS, CLOWNS, & GYPSIES** (ISBN 0-9631060-2-3) by Cap'n Fatty Goodlander at $8.50 + $1.50 for P&H.

****

Please send me _____ copies of **CHASING THE HORIZON** (ISBN 0-9631060-1-5) by Cap'n Fatty Goodlander at $10.50 plus a $1.50 each for postage and handling.

Chasing the Horizon is a delightfully demented Celebration of A Way of Life. It is an outrageously funny, often touching, and continuously shocking tale of a modern sea gypsy.

Cap'n Fatty's story is too bizarre to be fiction. Father wears floral skirts; mother is a tad vague. Sister Carole isn't interested in her millionaire suitor; she's too busy smooching with the kid in the cesspool truck. Their strange live-aboard boat caravan includes Mort the Mortician, Backwards Bernie, Ruby Red the Conman, Barefoot Benny, Geeper Creeper, Para the Paranoid, Lusty Laura, Xlax, Shark Boy, the Pawtucket Pirate, Bait Broad, Colonel Crispy, Scupper Lips, Bob the Broker, the Pirate Queen, Otto the Owner, the Twin Slaves of Green Slime-- and even a terribly long-winded fellow named (Hurricane) Hugo. All seem hell-bent on avoiding the cops, the creeps, each other, and especially the Dreaded Dream Crushers.

****

I've ordered a total of _____ books, and enclosed a check or money order payable to AMERICAN PARADISE PUBLISHING for the amount of _____.

Name_____

Address_____

_____

_____Zip_____

Mail to: American Paradise Publishing, POB 37, Cruz Bay, St. John, USVI 00831   (Allow four weeks for delivery)